Lerner SPORTS

SPORTS

VIPs

T0015627

MEET
NIKOLA JOKIĆ

DAVID STABLER

Lerner Publications ◆ Minneapolis

SPORTS THRILLS
MEET
RESEARCH SKILLS

Lerner SPORTS

Free Database Trial: **lernersports.com**

Lerner Publications Company
An imprint of Lerner Publishing Group, Inc.
241 First Avenue North
Minneapolis, MN 55401 USA

For reading levels and more information, look up this title at www.lernerbooks.com.

Main body text set in Aptifer Slab LT Pro. Typeface provided by Linotype AG.

Editor: Annie Zheng **Photo Editor:** Nicole Berglund

Library of Congress Cataloging-in-Publication Data

Names: Stabler, David, author.
Title: Meet Nikola Jokić : Denver Nuggets superstar / David Stabler.
Description: Minneapolis : Lerner Publications , [2024] | Series: Lerner Sports. Sports VIPs | Includes bibliographical references and index. | Audience: Ages 7–11 years | Audience: Grades 4–6 | Summary: "Center Nikola Jokić is a triple-double machine and a two-time NBA MVP. In 2016, he led Team Serbia to silver at the Olympic Games. Explore his life on and off the court"—Provided by publisher.
Identifiers: LCCN 2023020721 (print) | LCCN 2023020722 (ebook) | ISBN 9798765624104 (lib. bdg.) | ISBN 9798765624166 (pbk.) | ISBN 9798765624180 (epub)
Subjects: LCSH: Jokić, Nikola, 1995– —Juvenile literature. | Centers (Basketball)—Serbia—Biography—Juvenile literature. | Basketball players—Serbia—Biography—Juvenile literature. | Denver Nuggets (Basketball team)—History—Juvenile literature. | National Basketball Association—History—Juvenile literature. | Basketball—United States—History—Juvenile literature.
Classification: LCC GV884.J65 S73 2024 (print) | LCC GV884.J65 (ebook) | DDC 796.323092 [B]—dc23/eng/20230627

LC record available at https://lccn.loc.gov/2023020721
LC ebook record available at https://lccn.loc.gov/2023020722

Manufactured in the United States of America
1-1009643-51855-8/2/2023

TABLE OF CONTENTS

>>>>>>>>>>>>>>

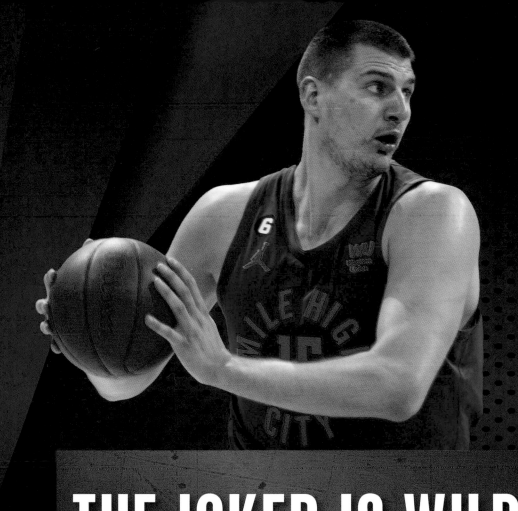

THE JOKER IS WILD

On January 19, 2022, the Denver Nuggets were locked in a tight contest against the Los Angeles Clippers. Nikola "the Joker" Jokić was the National Basketball Association's (NBA) reigning Most Valuable Player (MVP). The Nuggets' star center scored on dunks and layups throughout the game. At the end of the fourth quarter, he had recorded 38 points. But the game was tied. The teams headed to overtime.

Jokić scored another 11 points in the overtime period for a total of 49. When he couldn't score, he passed to open teammates or grabbed rebounds to make a fast break down the court.

FAST FACTS

DATE OF BIRTH: February 19, 1995
POSITION: center
LEAGUE: NBA

PROFESSIONAL HIGHLIGHTS: won the 2023 NBA Championship; named NBA MVP in 2021 and 2022; scored over 100 triple-doubles in his career

PERSONAL HIGHLIGHTS: nicknamed the Joker; bought his first racehorse in 2016; married his longtime girlfriend, Natalija Mačešić, in 2020

Jokić passes the ball past Clippers defenders.

    With 8.7 seconds left in overtime, the game was tied once more. But then Jokić made a tricky cross-court pass to teammate Aaron Gordon. Gordon caught the pass and let the ball fly. It swished through the net. The Nuggets won 130–128!

    The last-second pass was Jokić's 10th assist for the game. In addition to his assists and points, he had 14 rebounds. That game, Jokić had earned a triple-double. He had double figures in three important stats.

In his time in the NBA, Jokić has racked up more than 100 triple-doubles. He is only the sixth player in history to do so. Whether it's offense, defense, passing, or rebounding—the Joker can do it all.

Jokić dribbles the ball near the basket as Clippers defender Brandon Boston Jr. tries to stop him.

CHAPTER 1

SERBIAN SENSATION

Nikola Jokić was born in Sombor, a small town in the eastern European nation of Serbia, on February 19, 1995. He grew up in a tiny apartment with his parents, grandmother, and two older brothers, Nemanja and Strahinja. Both of his brothers excelled at playing basketball. As a baby, Nikola would watch his brothers shoot hoops while he sat on his father's lap.

The boys sometimes played with a toy basketball hoop that hung over a door in their home. When Nikola was little, his brothers would sit on the floor and teach him how to make shots in the toy hoop. As he got better at it, Nikola started making dunks and layups. The boys' games got so loud and heated that downstairs neighbors would come up to complain about the noise.

Nikola shows off his jersey in 2018 after signing a new contract with the Denver Nuggets. *Left to right*: His brother Nemanja Jokić; Nikola Jokić; his then girlfriend and later wife, Natalija Mačešić; and brother Strahinja Jokić.

Nikola leads his horse back to its stall in a stable.

When Nikola was older, he found another sport he liked almost as much as basketball: horse racing. One day his father took him to a horse race in Sombor. After the race, he asked his dad if they could go visit the stables to get a closer look at the animals. "And I just fell in love with the horses," Nikola said.

Nikola started working with horses. He even rode in a competition. "Our stable, we were like a club," he said. "We raced some professionals. But I wasn't professional. I was just amateur." In his first and only race, Nikola took fourth place, beating out riders with much more experience than he had.

As good as he was at racing, Nikola realized that basketball was still his best sport, in part because of his

SUPER SPORTS SCOOP

Jokić never lost his love for horses. In 2016, he bought his first racehorse, Dream Catcher. He owns six horses and runs his own stable in Serbia when he isn't playing basketball.

Nikola Jokić stands 6 feet 11 (2.1 m). He talks to Atlanta Hawks guard Trae Young, who stands 6 feet 1 (1.8 m), during a game in 2021.

height. A horse racer benefits from being small so the horse has less weight to carry. But a basketball player's height can help them reach high to grab rebounds and shoot over shorter players. And Nikola was very tall. When it was time to take school photos, he usually had to lie down to fit inside the frame.

Nikola began to take basketball more seriously when he was a teenager. He studied YouTube videos of NBA stars such as Michael Jordan and Kobe Bryant to see what made them great. In 2012, Nikola joined a Serbian youth basketball league. His size and skill soon began drawing interest from other teams.

When Nikola was 17, Mega Vizura, a team in Belgrade, Serbia, offered him a chance to play for them. Nikola packed up his things and left home to join the Adriatic League, a pro basketball league in eastern Europe. It was the first stop on his road to the NBA.

Nikola (*right*) guards a player in the Adriatic League during a 2013 game.

BELGRADE AND BEYOND

Before Jokić could start playing for his new team, he first had to get into playing shape. The Mega Vizura coaches worried that he was too weak to compete against stronger players. He spent most of his first season in a special training program to help him build muscle.

By his second season in Belgrade, Jokić was in better shape. Coaches put him in the starting lineup. He averaged 11.4 points, 6.4 rebounds, and two assists per game. Those stats caught the attention of scouts from the NBA.

Jokić (*center*) stops a rival player in the Adriatic League.

On the night Jokić (*right*) was drafted, he was fast asleep in Serbia. He played his first season with the Denver Nuggets in 2015.

On June 26, 2014, the Denver Nuggets picked Jokić with the 41st overall pick in the NBA Draft. After getting drafted by the Nuggets, Jokić stayed in Serbia for one final season in the Adriatic League. He ended the season on a high by earning MVP honors. The center looked forward to starting the next chapter of his career in the NBA.

To prepare, Jokić began working out at the Nuggets training center before the new season. He also began eating healthier food. His brothers and his girlfriend moved to Denver, Colorado, to give him support. By the time the new season rolled around, Jokić was ready to take on the NBA.

SUPER SPORTS SCOOP

Jokić's former Nuggets teammate Mike Miller had trouble saying Jokić's last name at first. So Miller gave Jokić a nickname: the Joker. Jokić is pronounced *YO-kitch*.

Jokić defends against Toronto Raptors player Jonas Valančiūnas.

All that hard work paid off as Jokić enjoyed a strong rookie season with the Nuggets. On February 1, 2016, he recorded career highs of 27 points and 14 rebounds in a 112–93 win over the Toronto Raptors. At the season's end, he finished third in voting for Rookie of the Year and earned All-Rookie First Team honors. The long road from Serbia to the NBA was over, but Jokić's road to superstardom was just beginning.

CHAPTER 3

MVP! MVP!

Nikola Jokić's rookie season was a success. But there was still room for improvement. In 2017, Jokić finished his second NBA season with six triple-doubles and was second in voting for the Most Improved Player Award. In 2018, he scored 30 points or more seven times. And in 2019, he made the NBA All-Star team, a team made up of the top-ranked NBA players.

Jokić puts up a shot against San Antonio Spurs player LaMarcus Aldridge.

That year, he also helped the Nuggets reach the NBA playoffs for the first time in six seasons. In Game 7 of their playoff series against the San Antonio Spurs, Jokić scored 21 points, 15 rebounds, and 10 assists to lead Denver to victory.

The Nuggets returned to the playoffs in 2020. This time, they faced the Los Angeles Clippers. Denver fell behind three games to one, but they roared back to tie the series. In Game 7, Jokić recorded a triple-double with 16 points, 22 rebounds, and 13 assists to help Denver win 104–89. The Nuggets went on to lose the Western Conference Finals to the Los Angeles Lakers.

SUPER SPORTS SCOOP

In October of 2020, Jokić married his longtime girlfrlend, Natalija Mačešić, in his hometown of Sombor. Their daughter, Ognjena, was born in September of 2021.

In the 2020–2021 season, Jokić got off to a hot start and never looked back. He began the season with four triple-doubles in his first six games. He finished the season averaging 26.4 points, 10.8 rebounds, and 8.3 assists per game. To top it off, Jokić won the NBA MVP Award for the first time. He was the first center to win the award since Shaquille O'Neal in 2000.

Jokić accepts the 2021 NBA MVP Award.

Jokić is defended by three Golden State Warriors players, including Draymond Green (*bottom left*).

Jokić won a second MVP Award in 2022. But it was his playoff performance that really caught the attention of NBA fans. In the first round of playoffs, the Denver Nuggets played the Golden State Warriors. Draymond Green, one of the league's best defensive players, was guarding Jokić. Despite this, Jokić scored 30 points or more in three out of five games. In Game 5, Jokić scored 12 of his 30 points in the final four minutes of the game.

After the game, Green pulled Jokić aside to congratulate him on a great series. "I told him thank you for making me better," Green said. "He's an absolutely incredible player."

CHAPTER 4

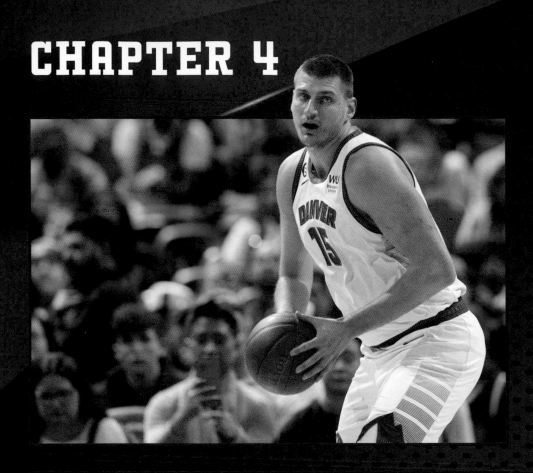

WHAT'S NEXT?

In the 2022–2023 season, Jokić picked up right where he left off the year before. He finished the season averaging 24.5 points and 9.8 assists per game. The Nuggets won 53 games and were a favorite to win the Western Conference playoffs.

After winning the first three rounds, the Nuggets met the Miami Heat in the NBA Finals. Jokić set the pace for his team in a fierce five-game series. He knocked down big shots, dished out key passes, and grabbed tough rebounds that kept Miami from scoring. Scoring more than 30 points a game, he was the key to Denver's victory over Miami. The Nuggets became NBA champions for the first time in team history. Jokić was named the NBA Finals MVP.

Jokić lifts up the NBA Finals MVP Award with his daughter, Ognjena.

SUPER SPORTS SCOOP

On July 1, 2022, Jokić signed a new five-year $264 million contract with the Nuggets. This makes him one of the highest-paid players in NBA history.

The Serbian sensation is proud of his skills. His best move is a one-legged jump shot. Fans call it the Sombor Shuffle after his hometown. This jump shot is considered one of the most unstoppable moves in the NBA.

But Jokić is equally proud of his ability to dish out assists to his teammates. "If I could score 40 every game, then I would score 40 every game," Jokić said. "But I think I cannot score 40 every game, so I'm gonna pass a little bit too."

With a wife, a young daughter, and a stable full of horses to care for, the Joker has a lot to look forward to. With an NBA title to celebrate, Nikola Jokić will truly be remembered as one of basketball's all-time legends.

Jokić rides through Denver on top of a fire truck with his daughter during the Denver Nuggets 2023 Champions Parade.

NIKOLA JOKIĆ CAREER STATS

GAMES PLAYED:

596

POINTS PER GAME:

20.2

REBOUNDS PER GAME:

10.5

ASSISTS PER GAME:

6.6

BLOCKS PER GAME:

0.7

Stats are accurate through the 2022–2023 NBA regular season.

GLOSSARY

assist: a pass from a teammate that leads directly to a score

contract: a written agreement, often between an athlete and a team

draft: when teams take turns choosing new players

dunk: a shot in basketball made by jumping high into the air and throwing the ball down through the basket

jump shot: a shot in basketball made by jumping into the air and releasing the ball with one or both hands at the peak of the jump

layup: a basketball shot made from near the basket usually by playing the ball off the backboard

rebound: grabbing and controlling the ball after a missed shot

reign: to hold a title

rookie: a first-year player

scout: a person who judges the skills of athletes

stable: a building in which animals, such as horses, are sheltered and fed

stat: a measurable category in basketball, such as games played, games started, number of assists, rebounds, or points

SOURCE NOTES

10 Nick Kosmider, "'Magnificent Creatures': How Nikola Jokic Found Peace in His Love for Horses," Athletic, March 19, 2020, https://theathletic.com/1685649/2020/03/19/magnificent -creatures-how-nikola-jokic-found-peace-in-his-love-of -horses/.

11 Franklyn Calle, "No Joke," *Slam*, December 20, 2016, https:// www.slamonline.com/news/nba/nikola-Jokic-nuggets -interview/.

23 Joey Linn, "Draymond Green Reveals What He Told Nikola Jokić after Game 5," *Sports Illustrated*, April 28, 2022, https:// www.si.com/nba/warriors/news/draymond-green-reveals -what-he-told-nikola-jokic-after-game-5.

26 Howard Beck, "The Way of the Joker," Bleacher Report, November 1, 2017, https://bleacherreport.com/articles/2741818 -the-way-of-the-joker-nikola-jokic.

LEARN MORE

Cain, Harold P. *Nikola Jokić: Basketball Star*. Lake Elmo, MN: Focus Readers, 2023.

Coleman, Ted. *Denver Nuggets All-Time Greats*. Mendota Heights, MN: Press Box Books, 2023.

Jr. NBA
https://jr.nba.com/

Kiddle: Basketball Facts for Kids
https://kids.kiddle.co/Basketball

Scheff, Matt. *NBA and WNBA Finals: Basketball's Biggest Playoffs*. Minneapolis: Lerner Publications, 2021.

Sports Illustrated Kids: Basketball
https://www.sikids.com/basketball

INDEX

PHOTO ACKNOWLEDGMENTS

Image credits: AP Photo/David Zalubowski, pp. 4, 9, 19, 24; Isaiah Vazquez/
Clarkson Creative/Getty Images, pp. 6, 7; xbrchx/Shutterstock, p. 8; Srdjan
Stevanovic/Getty Images, p. 10; Todd Kirkland/Getty Images, p. 12; Marko
Prpic/Pixsell/Alamy, pp. 13, 15; AAron Ontiveroz/The Denver Post/Getty
Images, pp. 14, 18, 25; San Francisco Chronicle/Hearst Newspapers/Getty
Images, p. 16; Matthew Stockman/Getty Images, p. 20; Dustin Bradford/
Stringer/Getty Images, p. 22; AP Photo/Jed Jacobsohn, p. 23; RJ Sangosti/
MediaNews Group/The Denver Post/Getty Images, p. 27. Design elements:
The Hornbills Studio/Shutterstock.

Cover: AP Photo/David Zalubowski.